PHONICS CONNECTIONS

Healthy You!

by Cass Hollander

Table of Contents

Keeping Fit 2
Exercise and Fitness 4
Food and Fitness. 8
Fitness for Life 12
Index 16

capstone classroom

Keeping Fit

What do you do to stay healthy? Do you make sure your body is in good physical condition? Keeping fit isn't just for grown-ups. Kids need to keep fit too.

Keeping fit helps you right now.
It will help you when you grow up too.
Kids who are healthy usually become healthy adults.

Exercise and Fitness

Exercise is important for fitness. You don't have to be on a sports team to get exercise. You don't have to do sit-ups or push-ups. Just playing on the playground or at your own home is a great way to get exercise.

There are many things you could do to stay healthy. You could climb a hill or slide down a slide. You could ride a bike or skate to school. You could even dance to a favorite tune. You could play with friends or play alone. The important thing is to move!

Cut down on

Watching TV & Videos
playing videos and computer games, sitting for more than 30 minutes at a time

2–3 times a week

Leisure & Playtime
miniature golf, canoeing, swinging, jumping

3–5 times a week

Aerobic Exercises
(at least 20 minutes)
biking, swimming, in-line skating, jumping rope, skateboarding, running around

Every day!
(as much as possible)

playing outside, riding your bike or walking to the store, walking your dog, helping around the house

You should try to eat a lot of fruits and vegetables. These foods have vitamins your body needs. Vitamins help you stay healthy by giving you energy to play and grow.

Fitness for Life

Keeping fit helps you build strong muscles. You need muscles to move every part of your body.

The more you use your muscles, the stronger they get. If you don't use your muscles enough, they can get weak and flabby.

Strong muscles aren't just for lifting heavy things. They help you bend and jump. They help you walk and run. They help your body do what you want it to do.

Keeping fit builds strong bones too. You need strong bones to grow straight and tall. You need strong bones to play hard. Strong bones help keep you healthy.

Sometimes as people get older, their bones can get thin and weak. But this doesn't have to happen. Exercise and healthful eating can help your bones stay strong your whole life.

Index

bones, 14–15

eating, 8–11, 15

exercise, 4, 6–7, 15

fats, 10

foods, 8–11

fruits, 11

moving, 5–7, 12

muscles, 12–13

playing, 4–7, 11, 13–14

sugars, 10

vegetables, 11

vitamins, 11